PLATFORM PAPERS

QUARTERLY ESSAYS ON THE PERFORMING ARTS

IIIIIIIIIIIIIIIIIIIIIIIIIIIIIIIIIIII

No. 24
July 2010

CURRENCY HOUSE

PLATFORM PAPERS
Quarterly essays from Currency House Inc.

Editor: Dr John Golder, j.golder@unsw.edu.au

Currency House Inc. is a non-profit association and resource centre advocating the role of the performing arts in public life by research, debate and publication.

Postal address: PO Box 2270, Strawberry Hills, NSW 2012, Australia

Email: info@currencyhouse.org.au   Tel: (02) 9319 4953
Website: www.currencyhouse.org.au   Fax: (02) 9319 3649

Editorial Board: Katharine Brisbane AM, Dr John Golder, John McCallum, Martin Portus, Greig Tillotson

ISBN 978-0-9805632-8-3
ISSN 1449-583X
Typeset in 10.5 Arrus BT
Printed by Hyde Park Press, Richmond, SA
Avatar image by Kathy Pope

This edition of Platform Papers is supported by the Greatorex Foundation, Neil Armfield, David Marr, Joanna Murray-Smith, Martin Portus and other individual donors and advisers. To them and to all our supporters Currency House extends sincere gratitude.

Contents

AVAILABILITY *Platform Papers*, quarterly essays on the performing
arts, is published every January, April, July and October and is
available through bookshops or by subscription. For order form,
see page 70.

LETTERS Currency House invites readers to submit letters of
400–1,000 words in response to the essays. Letters should be
emailed to the Editor at info@currencyhouse.org.au or posted to
Currency House at PO Box 2270, Strawberry Hills, NSW 2012,
Australia. To be considered for the next issue, the letters must be
received by 16 August 2010.

CURRENCY HOUSE For membership details, see our website at:
www.currencyhouse.org.au

The Digital Playing Fields:

New rulz for film, art and performance

SHILO McCLEAN

The author

Shilo McClean is the author of the books: *Digital Storytelling: the narrative power of visual effects in film* (MIT Press, 2007) and *So What's This All About Then: a non-user's guide for digital effects in film* (AFTRS, 1998). In April 2008 she was keynote speaker for the Norwegian Film Institute's Digital Storytelling Conference and jury member for the Norwegian Best Visual Effects awards. In June 2008, she was the keynote speaker for Framework: create, an event and forum for games and convergent industries. Recent papers and lectures include: 'Building Bridges, Not Falling Through Cracks: what we've learned from ten years of Australian DVFx Traineeships' (SIGGRAPH 2009); *Children of the e•volution: the curator's role in the user-led content revolution* (CPRF 2006); *Mapping the 'Verse: three case studies identifying emerging models of user-generated content* (CPRF 2007); *Resourcing School: re-thinking education in a connected world* (CPRF 2008); and *FutureYou: documentary in a YouTube world* (Film Australia/ScreenWest Doco2012 Conference, 2008).

Shilo designs and conducts seminars, workshops, and lectures for industry and tertiary courses in film-making, digital visual effects and storycraft. She is a consultant to the Screen NSW Visual Effects Scheme, Vice Chair of Sydney ACM SIGGRAPH and was

Digital Strand Curator for the 2006 and 2007 Sydney Film Festivals, producing and directing a series of podcasts for the Festival site in 2006 and was a pre-selector for the Dendy Awards in 2009.

Her film credits include: *Out* (1994), *Smoked Oysters* (1995), *The Beat Manifesto* (1995), *Dreaming of Freedom* (1996), *The Zipper* (1998), *The Tichborne Claimant* (1998), *Desire Lines* (1999), *How Long Is A Piece Of String* (2002), and *Adding Strings To Your Bow* (2003).

Acknowledgements

I know that I have yet to meet many of the wonderful people who will be due great thanks and acknowledgement in the time that lies ahead in getting this Platform Paper out and into the debate, and so my first thanks are to those who have helped it on its way. I look forward to meeting you all and thanking you in person.

For making this essay happen in the first place, I thank Greg Smith for introducing me to John Golder and Katharine Brisbane, and I thank them for their welcome and their openness; I knew we would hit it off when they agreed to using my online avatar image on the back cover, instead of a more traditional photograph. As we worked together, I found myself adding my voice to the chorus of praise by authors who have benefitted from working with John's editorial eye. His pen is deft and light, adding and subtracting with admirable precision.

I want to thank Currency House also for its commitment to debate and fresh ideas. When I read *The Girl with the Dragon Tattoo*, I thought that the offices of Millennium would be a great place to work in and I think, in Currency House, I have found that same kind of courage and intellectual rigour. I take my hat off to them for all they achieve.

Some introductory remarks

Whereas rules can be about setting standards for conformity, I want to argue the case for claiming ownership, because I believe that the digital playing fields offer not only competition, but opportunity—a chance to w00t[1] in the most creative way. In the discussion that follows, 'rulz' means to win and own; to take over new territory.

My entrée into the ranks of the digital was serendipitous. Twenty years ago, a chance encounter with the latest developments in computer graphics for film convinced me that computer graphics were a valuable storytelling tool. In my view, the enrichment of storytelling through the narrative use of computer graphics is one of the great benefits of computerisation. Not everyone agrees with this: many argue that 'all this digital stuff' is cold and hard. People often assert that digital imagery is obvious and that their use drains warmth from narratives. Furthermore, these views are not confined to computer graphics in films, for many, digital tools are at odds with the humanity that should be at the core of 'real' art forms.

There is nothing like the threat of the new to draw nay-sayers like seagulls to a hot chip. In the mid-1990s, when I wanted to make a short computer-generated film, I faced opposition from every quarter. It was too expensive, they said, and computer graphics weren't very good because no-one knew how to do them properly. Many argued that computer-generated films weren't 'real' films and it was clear they hoped that if they said this enough it would make this new technology go away. I was not persuaded by these arguments. On graduating from the Australian Film, Television and Radio School (AFTRS), I decided to find out what filmmakers needed to know if they wanted to use computer graphics. The research I undertook, supported by the AFTRS Kenneth Myer Fellowship, resulted in a book, *So What's This All About Then: a non-user's guide to digital effects in filmmaking.*[2] (It has been updated for Screen Australia's *Satchel.*[3]) Not only did I want to refute the nay-saying, I wanted others to do it, too.

As a consequence, I was looked upon as 'one of those digital people' and wound up in endless discussions with those who wanted to persuade me that computer graphics were ruining films. Incensed by these arguments, I wrote *Digital Storytelling: the narrative power of visual effects in film.*[4] The focus of this book is classic feature-film narratives and how visual effects have expanded narrative tools for filmmakers. However, as I wrote it, I found myself taking up the wider cause of emerging narrative experiences—and it is with these that I want to engage in this essay.

The changes we have seen have happened so quickly that there is a tendency for people to conflate all things digital. On my website I have the tagline,

'Digital doesn't mean I can fix your computer'. Although my interest is computer graphics, I find myself consulted on digital sound, digital editing, digital photography, email, how to use the Microsoft suite of applications... while at the same time having to listen to rants about how access to the Internet means the end of civilisation as we know it. And yes, in spite of the tagline, I still get asked to fix computers.

Most often the arguments I encounter about digital technologies arise out of fear about what these changes will bring, even though the impact of these technologies across almost every form of human endeavour heralds profound—and largely positive— change. I am particularly persuaded by how we are using them to enhance the way we tell stories. I love storytelling. It is one of the cleverest, most important things we analogue creatures do, and we are on the cusp of being able to realise story in ways that we have always yearned to do. Fundamental to this is the fact that the technologies we are developing through our use of digital tools will allow audiences to experience stories in ways that work best for them and allow them to be active participants in the story.

Storytelling has always been a means of passing on knowledge and wisdom. It is a vital link from one generation to the next. It is one of the ways in which we make sense of ourselves. To our great good fortune, though wind may have scoured the stone on which our earliest stories were recorded and many a great library has been lost to fire and human conflict, stories have endured. Endurance is their mission and redundancy and reinvention are vital to their survival. Given the means to do so, a story lost in one place will rise again elsewhere. As we develop new technologies, we can reinvent our stories for future generations. Our new tools suit these purposes marvellously well.

1

The state of play

What happened when those unknown artists sketched images of the hunt on the cave walls at Lascaux? Was there someone behind them, warning that if they continued to paint these scenes the kids would lose the ability to hunt, and then the whole tribe would starve? Or, as Walter Benjamin put it, was their painting seen as an instrument of magic, to be held in fearful reverence?

There is something about art and performance that draws upon our fears, and perhaps this is what incites our desire to control, to regulate, to mediate and, yes, to censor. Whatever the medium, be it images, live performance or literary narrative, the aim is the expression and communication of emotions and ideas. It is an onerous task, and it is not hard to see why, throughout history, the privileged few have sought to use the power conferred by innovative technology to control the many.

Nonetheless, talent, imagination and creativity cannot be corralled by conformity and the predictable. Ingenuity will have its way. History teems with creative revolutions, often linked to technological advances and, no less often, it is technology itself that is said to have brought them about. Certainly, digital technologies are blamed today for many of the changes currently taking place. However, as history has shown, technological determinism is rarely an adequate explanation for social change.

In his *Technologies of Seeing*, Brian Winston traces the development of visual technologies and the factors responsible for their success and deployment: the desire to establish monopolies over technology; the biases that influence the direction of technological development; and the need to accommodate social demands. '[I]n the dance of history', he writes, 'society always leads technology'.[5] Broadly stated, Winston's argument is that it is social forces that motivate the adoption of technology, and that the scientific discoveries underpinning it, have usually existed in some form or another before the enabling technology is engineered to respond.

It is what happens next, once technologies are adopted, that is crucial to the extent to which their potential will be realised. It is an established pattern that innovation is followed by commercial exploitation, which eventually trends to situations of monopoly or oligopoly in the control of production. The pattern is so common one might even think it inevitable. Indeed, it could be argued that the ensuing stagnation that arises once a field is dominated by powerbrokers is, in fact, a condition that is a prerequisite for further innovation. Yet this cycle of change must keep moving and if stability is allowed to become stagnation it can hold back new standards and tools, which is exactly what happens if there are insufficient means to counter the dead hand of dominant players.

Certainly this is what has happened in the film industry. While most would measure the industry by the technological advances of the last hundred years, Winston traces the industry from the Chinese magic lantern of 121 BCE and the *camera obscura* of the 1500s. He notes that these innovations were only adopted and developed into the film technologies of the 1900s once syndicated theatre and vaudeville had provided them with mass audiences in the large urban communities created by the Industrial Revolution. It was at that point that the social needs arising from this change made cinema inevitable.

David Bordwell, a rigorous researcher of the cinema's industrial practices, has tracked the way in which film's narrative form was locked down as early as 1917 and survived through the studio system of the inter- and post-War decades to the vertically integrated multi-national interests of the present day.[6] He and other historians have documented the ways in which repeated cycles of change have led to moments of independence and innovation that have been overcome by market forces and corporate strategies.

In *The Way Hollywood Tells It*, Bordwell describes the fraught state of the film business in the last third of the twentieth century, as film attendances fell and the studios had to rely on lucrative deals with television to survive. Having lost their theatre chains, studios began, as he puts it, to 'haemorrhage money'. Tax schemes, the increasing vertical integration of media and telecommunications companies, the spread of multiplexes and merchandising—all played their part in the industry's recovery. However, Bordwell says, '[it was the sales of] DVDs [that] were keeping virtually every movie's budget afloat.'[7] Ironically, even though they were initially perceived as a threat, television, video tapes and DVDs were eventually used as a means of controlling production, distribution and market position. Driven by their acquisition mentality, the major corporations spent the 1980s and '90s securing control over filmmaking and its related 'products' through publishing, television, theme parks and emerging digital platforms.[8]

These advances led to unexpected outcomes also. The availability of a vast back catalogue of films enabled a generation of filmmakers to study classic cinema from every corner of the globe in a way that scholars relying upon film prints could only have fantasised about. Screenwriting guides and film schools became boom business. It seemed that, finally, filmmaking was an open industry, one that could be entered by proving one's storytelling skills. Equipped with a wealth of filmmaking knowledge, a generation grew up with an expectation of being able to harness visual storytelling skills that were at one time exclusive to a small group of professionals.

As the title of Steven Soderbergh's film *Sex, Lies and Videotape* seemed to suggest, film was hot. For a brief and golden time there was a mother lode of independently made, low-budget films. Most famously perhaps, *El Mariachi* opened theatres on the basis that it was made for only $7,000, inspiring everyone with a credit card and a script.

In the independent documentary *American Movie*, director Chris Smith captures what almost feels like a parody of the guerrilla filmmaking that ensued at the time. In the film, his subject—filmmaker Mark Borchardt, explains to his Uncle Bill (the film's main investor), 'I only need to sell [a varying number] of units in order to recoup the investment.' When the elderly relative invests $3,000, the filmmakers proceed in a manner not unlike that documented in Joe Queenan's book, *The Unkindest Cut*, an account of his *El Mariachi*-inspired auteur project, *Twelve Steps to Death*. In the early 1990s, the guerrilla filmmaking phenomenon was so pervasive that Queenan, a film critic known for his caustic humour, felt compelled to try his own hand at filmmaking and discovered first hand the challenge that independent filmmaking represents.

Enabling this phenomenon, advances in digital technologies put professional-standard equipment in the hands of 'amateurs'; a whole suite of digital tools not only became available, but affordable also. The magnitude of the change was profound. For example, in the mid-1990s the price of an entry-level workstation with a powerful graphics card ranged from AU$10,000 up to around $60,000. Licences for these machines also cost thousands of dollars and, as the capabilities of the software increased almost weekly, they needed to be kept current. Just to stay in the game required a major investment.

Similarly in 1994, burning a CD cost AU\$30 for the blank disc and about \$100 for the service. The burner itself cost AU\$12,000. A decade later, every stage of this process could be undertaken with consumer electronics and a home computer. Today, a blank CD or DVD retails for as little as 10 to 50 cents. On a professional level also, the higher-end versions of these tools changed the equation for those creating work for trade markets. Where once film (and the associated costs for transfers and laboratory prints) set the standard, digital recording that linked directly to other digital processes—such as computer graphics and editing—gave people a less expensive way of making something that could prove a product's viability and raise funds needed to meet 'professional' market deliverables.

At roughly the same time, the Internet emerged from the realms of academic and military networks and into corporate and telecommunications networking. Within ten years, the novelty of personal email had morphed into an unparalleled level of global connectivity, offering video and data transfer at speeds and capacities that increase exponentially. YouTube, Flickr, Facebook, and a myriad of applications, put enormous power in the hands of virtually anyone with an idea and the will and talent to express it. Suddenly it seemed that anyone prepared to make their own stuff was in a position to craft and distribute it in a way that bypassed the traditional gatekeepers.

For the most part, however, the 'have laptop, will broadcast' generation seems to be regarded by traditional media sectors as either fodder for the 'tech' reports or as a threat that needs to be repelled. This generation's production of vast amounts of content without clear business models frustrates entrenched media powerbrokers that want to 'own' the space. The ability of 'Internet people' to attract attention—often by mocking 'old' media, while at the same time stealing audiences and undermining *real* business models—has sown seeds for real conflict. Increasingly, the entrenched media players are characterising many of the technologies that threaten their business models as ones that threaten wider social welfare. At the heart of these tactics is the intention to wrest the tools of production from those undermining the foundations of the status quo—that would be, from us.

Just as industrialisation concentrated audiences in urban centres, the electronics revolution and suburban growth created audiences in the home. Audiences that built media rooms and hardwired their houses to engage in that oldest of practices—enjoying storytelling. Very quickly, this same audience started making its own content once it had the means to do so.

Admittedly, very little of this production was meant for wide distribution. However, what these tools did offer was a means of practising filmcraft. Apprenticeships in production are harder to find today than they were even as recently as the 1990s. Due, in part, to an expectation that the skills and knowledge needed are part of general literacy, the level of experience needed at entry level is often quite high. There is an economic factor at play here also. The out-sourcing of production, the limited numbers of professional opportunities, and—thanks to a flourishing 'indie' market—a wealth of material on offer from those prepared to pay to work, mean that people are expected to ready themselves for the market rather than expect the market to provide them with the means by which to become skilled.

In spite of continual hype about the industry's successes, professional opportunities remain limited. Explaining why he was moving overseas to find work, a colleague recounted to me how his hopes were dashed when he heard that one of his heroes had taken a day job. It turned out that, even for someone with exceptional film credits, there were at least ten others, equally well-qualified, vying to work on the two or three studio-funded projects that came into Australia in any given year. It was simple mathematics: even if each was given a turn in some kind of 'fair go' system, they could only hope to be head of department every couple of years. Clearly, if the best in the business were hard-pressed to stay in paid work, there was little room for others trying to get their first break.

There is also the problem that, in a risk-averse industry, feeding the vertically-integrated media-telecommunications merchandising machine is at the top of any decision-making agenda. Those projects that do receive funding comply with a fairly narrow set of criteria. Furthermore, there is an expectation that any venture has to be able to guarantee success, a requirement that, almost by nature, does not engender creativity and innovation. It is not a promising environment for new voices, unless they can find alternative outlets, be they through new forms or new ways of using old forms. As it turns out, there is a generation whose belief is that their voice *has a right* to be heard.

Despite our fears of change, we crave innovation, and that is enough to inspire us to overcome our fears and find new ways to create. It is this desire to *make things* that has been most powerful in advancing the technologies that drive our current progress in the creative arts. Yet the urge of the traditional media and telecommunications industries to control these technologies is becoming stronger every day. Need we let this happen yet again? The only way we can prevent the dominant players from tipping the playing field to their own advantage is to oppose them with force as strong as theirs. Thanks to the Internet, we have the numbers on our side.

In the 1980s and '90s, the nascent digital revolution seemed set to overturn the oligopoly in content production. Twenty years later, however, as Janet Wasko has pointed out, eight companies still receive 95 per cent of all box-office revenue, and three quarters of the overseas market is controlled by US studios.[9] That playing field continues to be tilted in favour of the few, and there is little to indicate that they are prepared to make way for any competition. Rupert Murdoch said recently, in relation to his plans to introduce paywalls for online content, 'I think when they've got nowhere else to go, they'll start paying.'[10] His remark sums up the situation well: for the entrenched players, not only is it about maintaining existing business models, it is about ensuring that no viable alternatives are able to arise outside of their control.

2

Changing stories

How does any of this impact on storytelling? Storytelling takes many forms, and these have fallen in and out of favour throughout history. At the time when stories were told aloud, committing them to paper was regarded as a way of killing them—of reducing them to dead words on a page. Radio resurrected the spoken story, but the filming of *written* stories met with considerable opposition. How could the playacting of a novel compare with the power of the written word? How were children to develop an active imagination, if they were simply the passive recipients of someone else's visual representation? An artist I interviewed recounted her son's reaction to the first *Harry Potter* film. An avid reader of J.K. Rowling's books, he watched the film quietly, and then, as he and his mother were leaving the cinema, he said, in a disappointed voice, 'Oh, so *that's* what Hagrid looks like.' Clearly, his imagined Hagrid was nothing like actor Robbie Coltrane, and so he assumed he had been wrong. Anecdotes of this kind highlight the very *personal* nature of story in our lives.

However, vital as this personal response is, for some time now the personal has been pushed aside by the 'provided' story. Children are less often told stories and more commonly are read to from published—and often, illustrated—works. While today we are exposed to innumerable narratives—and in more forms than ever before—it is only recently that we have been able to create and share our own versions of stories, thanks to the opportunities afforded in a digital world.

An old story must continue to find a new form in which to encode itself and be accepted by a changing society. For example, once upon a time the survival of a tribe depended, at least in part, on its willingness to accept outsiders and for individuals to embrace change, to find new places and peoples to belong to. Whether that story in its current iteration is *Pocahontas* or *Avatar* (which might be considered, 'Pocahontas in Space'), if the essence of that story resonates, it will find an audience.

The form best suited to ensure that a story *will* resonate, however, remains a matter of contention. Many hold that film can never have the psychological, descriptive or narrative complexity of novels. For others, films offer a narrative engagement that they simply never find in reading. Similarly, the argument is made that games cannot be as engaging as films because the player controls a narrative flow that is limited by the game design. However, the differences between these various narrative experiences do not elevate one form over the other: they simply demonstrate that there is a variety of ways of enjoying narrative, and that we are becoming increasingly interested in having our individual needs met by the various means available.

What does remain constant is the fact that that story, whatever form it takes, is an important means by which we learn to deal with our ever-changing world. The underpinnings of story are not its form—although there may be constants there, too—but the wisdom embedded within its evolving forms. Epic poems are not so popular with the kids these days, except perhaps when they come in the form of the movie *Beowulf* or when they read the 140-character limited language of Twitter in Penguin's *Twitterature* version which opens with the immortal lines: 'Just swam a whole river to settle a bet. Won, of course. Now this guy must sit on my horned helmet. A bet's a bet.'[11] (Isn't that how many readers with a classical education recall that famous epic's glorious opening?) Others will prefer the experience of being the hero in *Fable*, a role-playing game in which players assume the role of an orphan boy who realises his dream by becoming a hero, or *World of Warcraft*, the massive multi-player online game set in a fantasy world in which the player creates their own character.

As Bruno Bettelheim documented in his *Uses of Enchantment*, a child encountering a story will attempt to identify with a character in the simple question, 'Who am I in this story?'.[12] The richness of the storyworld and the dramatic power on offer are important qualities in our narrative experiences. The depth and variety of means by which stories can be expressed and enjoyed in a digitally-enhanced world are still being developed. One thing is clear, that the incentive for exploring the narrative world, connecting with it, and the resonance of the meanings that underpin it, are driven to a great extent by our social needs.

There are three significant ways in which stories can endure. They can be retold. They can be re-formed, that is, given a new narrative expression such as transformation from biblical legend to visual representation in the form of a painting. And they can also be 'owned', taken up and woven into the fabric of our identity. Through these means, stories can be extended and given refreshed life.

Filmmaking is a powerful means of telling stories. We appreciate that it combines various art forms, giving them an immediacy and intimacy that can be wonderfully persuasive. David Bordwell has described the worldmaking qualities of film and how this has been extended, as vertically integrated media-telecom practices have taken hold:

> *Star Wars* signalled the marketing potential of massive detailing. [...F]rom the outset this world spilled off the screen. [George] Lucas, who published a comic book and a novelization of *Star Wars* before the film was released, understood immediately that cross-media worldmaking was one way to extend the studio idea of a B-series. Audiences who had visited Disneyland and had seen comic-book characters become TV heroes were ready to enter a self-contained universe straddling many media. The richer the world, the more likely fans were to explore it.[13]

It is this 'readied audience' that we must consider. For the last fifty years, popular culture and its products have been permeating story forms in a deliberately self-referential way. Where once the classics were a familiar reference for our hero's quippy response, the back catalogue of film and television is the reference resource now. The process of incorporating these references is faster and more iterative than ever before. To many, this not only proves that pop will eat itself, but also that the self-referential insularity of popular entertainment provides further proof that nothing is original anymore.

It is a mistake to think this is a modern phenomenon, though. Stories have always travelled and been reworked to suit the popular forms of the day. Earlier this year Haisam Hussein published a map that documented the geographic and formic evolution of four enduring stories: Pygmalion, Faust, Oedipus and Leviathan.[14] The story of Oedipus is traced from an epic poem in 800BCE to three separate plays in Athens over a period of some sixty years (467–406BCE), then to Rome and a play by Julius Caesar in 50BCE, an epic poem by Ovid in 5CE, and a play by Seneca in 60CE. The story reappears in London, 1678 as a play by John Dryden before being reworked in Paris in 1827 as a painting by Ingres, then again (still in Paris) in 1864 as another painting, this time by Gustave Moreau. Sigmund Freud reinvents the story as a treatise in Vienna in 1899, before Yeats turns it into two plays in Dublin in 1926–27. Thirty years later, in Toronto, Tyrone Guthrie references both Sophocles and Yeats in his film version. In Los Angeles in 1966, the Doors turn it into the song entitled 'The End', and Japanese novelist Haruki Murakami revisits it in 2002 in his *Kafka on the Shore*. Most recently, like the earlier reference to Beowulf, it has been reprised globally in Penguin's *Twitterature*, 2009. (And, as John

Golder has pointed out for me, Hussein could have added five neo-classical French stage versions, written between 1681 and 1858.[15])

While this rather undermines the belief that it is only recently that we have become such 'unoriginal' storytellers, it underlines the fact that retelling and reforming constitute the very essence of story and that this is effected on many levels: in the original crafting of a work; again as the story is 'received', regardless of the form in which it is presented; and then again as it resides as a seed of an idea or image, influencing us as we go about our lives—sometimes re-emerging as our 'own' version.

This uptake blurs the boundaries of creative forms. Once upon a time, many of the paintings in art galleries were the storytelling form of their day. Through iconic images and the language of symbolism, they conveyed much to the image-literate audiences of their times, often in a language that needs translation for modern art gallery patrons. Today, however, that patron might buy a reproduction of an item that most impressed them, and modify the image for an online avatar, or as wallpaper for their desktop, or as the basis of a creative work of their own.

While this rising trend for exploitation may seem like crass commercialism, it exists and thrives because it meets a need, a need that has been nurtured in suburban homes, in the megaplexes, and in the imaginations of at least two generations of media-rich nations. These audiences want to 'own' the story.

These are audiences who decide that if they quite like the story, then they want the T-shirt to prove it.

Even better, they will make their own T-shirts and post the artwork online to share with others. Stories that are really loved will be re-enacted, such as the crowdsourced remake of *Star Wars—StarWars Uuncut*—in which individual scenes are cut into 15-second clips and remade by separate groups acting independently and then assembled into a 'new' version.[16] Some scenes are re-enacted in full costume, others are performed by dogs, LEGO characters and people wearing cardboard facemasks. True aficionados write their own versions based on favourite characters and story worlds, taking source narratives into completely new territory. Some of these revisions become originals in their own right, as in the case of Louis Bayard's novel *Mr Timothy*, about Dickens' Tiny Tim, who is now 23, living in a London brothel and trying to shake off the ghost of his late father, Bob Cratchit.

Where once upon a time children played out Westerns with toy handguns and chaps made from tea towels and shoelaces, today's children are playing *Indiana Jones* LEGO video games—on game levels they created within the game—recording 'their' version of the story and uploading it to YouTube.

Is this changing the nature of storytelling, or is it simply the way in which storytelling works? Some believe that it is the technology that is changing our stories, but, as Hussein's map of the Oedipus myth shows, we have always reworked stories and presented them again in new forms. The impetus to use whatever technologies we have at hand is driven by the expectation that those technologies will enable us to tell our version in a new, and better, way. As

Clay Shirky has noted, 'We are living in the middle of a remarkable increase in our ability to share, to cooperate with one another, and to take collective action, all outside the framework of traditional institutions and organizations.'[17] While many of our favourite narratives may have the benefit of corporate births, the lives they take on once they leave the nest are subject to many forces, including the influence of strangers.

It is clear from these developments that narrative need not be limited, neither by its form, nor by conventions that have been established in previous tellings. In traditional narrative formats, multiple plotlines and alternate versions of stories usually had to be drawn back into linear resolution and explained away as having been 'all just a dream'. This is no longer the case. Television series such as *Life on Mars*, *Heroes*—and, in particular, the never-ending, ever-changing *Dr Who*—demonstrate the extent of the freedoms that storytellers now have to take narrative into more ambiguous territory.

Furthermore, the silos of 'film', 'television', 'novel' and the now rather quaintly named 'video' game, are no longer as containing as they once were. A fluidity between forms and a leapfrogging of ideas allows games to become films, which in turn become graphic novels and so on and so forth. One thing informing this fluidity is the experience of game playing, which permits actions to be replayed with different outcomes. An audience experienced in the narrative of gameplay is one that is used to engagement that is open to creative exploration in a medium that codes self as performer and codes the narrative experience in 'my story' terms.

The cross-platforming of story and the opportunity to engage with it in so many ways make it harder to determine which version is the 'real' one. As in the case of Oedipus, there are a number of 'originals'. Which is it: the myth, the novel, the play script, the film script, the director's storyboard, the film as released, the director's cut, or the animatic? The film script, once solely an in-house production tool, is now likely to be published and sold as a reference for scriptwriters. The storyboard, also once a production tool, is now also likely to be published and sold in art-book form, while the originals go on a national tour of art galleries. The animatic that set the camera moves and action of the story in moving frames may now be recycled as a making-of DVD feature, and at the same time be part of an installation at the aforementioned art-gallery exhibits alongside the original storyboards. Or should we look to the novelisation and 'continuing adventures of' in books, graphic novels and community blogs, in which extensive re-workings and re-imaginings explore the fine details and backstory underpinning the story world? And what of the emerging hybrid forms that use various sources to create a new work such as the YouTube posting of onemoreuser@yandex. ru's reworking of the trailer for the feature film, *Law-Abiding Citizen* and the video game *Team Fortress 2*, in which live-action movie materials are 'mashed up' with footage from games to create something that is neither the game nor the trailer but, impeccably, a bit of both?[18]

Whether it is *Halo* the game, *Halo* the movie or the novel *Halo Evolutions: Essential Tales of the Halo Universe*, each of us is free to find our 'own' version that suits our narrative preferences. Moreover, the trend—as with the *Star Wars* novels, films, games and remakes—is for each of us to bring our own contribution to the story worlds that have significance for us and, in so doing, to create a narrative legacy that grows, snowball-like, as each new party participates in and retells the story.

This intense personal engagement offers storymakers wonderful opportunities. Digital platforms such as DVDs have made it possible for the story originators to enhance the narrative through complex layering and additional materials, secure in the knowledge that sophisticated viewers are likely to explore the material through multiple viewings and eke out the subtle cues in backgrounds and turns of phrase.

Once again, extensions of story for commercial benefits have unexpected outcomes. The digital tools that allow the extension of corporate, 'provided' stories also permit audiences to personalise them.

The fundamental human need to tell stories and to adopt them as 'our own' is currently enjoying a renaissance. However, this development is under challenge from those who do not want to share the fun, and it remains to be seen whether or not those of us who *do* want to share the fun will be able to refine the tools at our disposal and use them to their full potential.

3

Old questions
for new forms,
new forms for old
questions

Since 1997, I have worked with Screen NSW
(formerly the New South Wales Film &
Television Office) in a program that provides
a training placement in digital visual effects. A few
years ago, I was asked by a prospective applicant if
working at Animal Logic would give him the skills he
needed for his dream career in the games industry.
'It's just that film and TV', he elaborated, 'well, it's
a bit old fashioned.' His comment indicates that, for
some, there has been a reordering of the hierarchy of
narrative forms. I mention this, however, not because
I want to argue that film is dead, but to demonstrate
some of the ways in which expectations of narrative
are evolving.

About six years ago I participated in a media
lab involving some of the world's leading games
developers. At that time discussion centred on how
games could be made more filmic. Then, in 2008, I
spoke at a workshop designed to bring filmmakers
and games developers together. By then, the desire to
make games more like films had been satisfied and the

games designers were focussed instead on enhancing gameplay and the narrative qualities that were inherent in how the game was designed. My talk at this event, 'Framework: create', focused on the common story elements shared by film and games and the way in which these elements support the differing story expressions that can be crafted through film and game design. These elements— premise, character, the story world and sense of place, how the action unfolds, and the engagement experience—are fundamental to both kinds of stories. But there are differences, differences that storytellers find inspirational.

In August 2009, in New Orleans, I spoke at the ACM SIGGRAPH (Association for Computing Machinery: Special Interest Group—Graphics) conference, the premier international forum for advances in visual effects and interactive techniques. At one panel filmmaker Danny Bilson told how he became aware that the stories he was sharing with his friends, instead of being those he was writing for film or television, had become stories of his experiences in games; and how this insight triggered a turning point for him as a storyteller. His presentation, 'Screenwriting in Gamespace', examined the writing skills needed for these narratives and described the importance of storytelling through action, emphasising that it was about the emergent story, the story about what we do in the game.

In comparing film and game narratives, three aspects of games are particularly important. First, games privilege the player rather than the games designer. The player is the 'author' of the experience. Film and literary theorists have long argued about 'authorship', but when it comes to gameplay, the sense of the self as key actor translates to, and is reinforced by, the second aspect of interest: agency. Agency is the ability to act in the world, to exert influence on that world and what happens in it. In some respects this is one of the key differences between games and film. While we might choose to identify with the hero in a film narrative, in a game it is around *our* actions that the story unfolds, and it is we who make decisions that lead to story outcomes. Admittedly, the extent of agency differs from game to game. Some games are highly directed, while others are more open to player-directed engagement. Sometimes, in multi-player games, our agency is tied to that of others. Whatever restrictions are embedded in the game design, our power to act and to be responsible for outcomes that are the result of our actions is central to the experience. Agency is closely associated with the third important feature of game playing, immersion in the storyworld. This may be the most compulsive quality that story affords us: the longer we connect with a story, its world and its characters, the better its chances of becoming a part of us. While a novel might engage us over a few days and film for a few hours, games can offer hundreds of hours of deep immersion.

These three features are intimately related to the sense of ownership that people can feel for narratives that attract them, and are key to the direction that narrative is taking. They are the reason why games have become such an integral part of the narrative landscape. Reviewing two recently-released games, Jordan Dean argued:

Emotional intensity versus spontaneity, developer intent versus player agency—there's no winner in these 'conflicts', no matter what EA [Electronic Arts]'s marketing department or Activision's SEC filings tell you. In fact, they're not battles at all, but rather questions. Should storytelling come at the expense of gameplay? Should players be allowed to make choices that go against the developers' wishes? How much responsibility for 'Fun' lies in the hands of the developers, and how much at the feet of players?[19]

These questions arise because the games industry is still exploring its narrative form and doing so in a way that is attempting to fulfil its community's desire for agency. These developments in games feed back to filmmaking also.

The film industry is more a stable than a booming industry. In 1960, when the world population was just over three billion, movie attendances totalled 1.39 billion. Since then attendances have declined. In the last decade, during which the world population rose to between six and seven billion, attendances have averaged only around 1.5 billion.[20] People are still watching films in substantial numbers, but as an established form, film—like opera, ballet and theatre—is no longer the rising creative force it was a century ago. Today's 'new audiences', as well as enjoying classical forms of narrative, are playing games, and the games industry *is* growing.

According to the Games Developers Association of Australia, '[t]he video games industry is now double the size of the box office and more than 40 per cent larger than the movie disc industry in Australia.'[21] The worldwide revenue from games is estimated at around US$41.9 billion. Comparative figures for other segments of the entertainment industry are reported as US$10 billion for music, US$27 billion for movies, US$63 billion for books, and US$23 billion for DVDs (of which US$16 billion is for purchases of DVDs). In 2007, the US game market tripled, growing six per cent and garnering US$9.5 billion dollars in domestic revenues, putting it on a par with box-office takings for that year.[22]

While many imagine these audiences to be comprised of young boys wasting their teenage years killing computer-generated characters, the reality is that the average age of gamers is over 30 years and they are playing a vast range of games. Moreover, 40 per cent of players today are women, and more females play games than teenage boys. One of the reasons for this growth is that games offer complex worlds that require knowledge of the game's environment, its story, and the player's own past actions within that narrative. Increasingly, players are able to design much of the experience themselves and to influence the story accordingly. Games also offer a meaningful connection with narrative that, like film, can be enjoyed as a communal or as a individual engagement.

For some, games can be more visually engaging than films, which, by comparison, can feel 'flat'. Game environments benefit from the highest production standards, often created by designers who have trained in architecture and fine arts. Further, the gamer's experience is enhanced by the sense of being able to move within these visually compelling environments.

Many of the reviews for the film *Avatar* (which won Academy Awards for its visual effects, cinematography and art direction) spoke of the immersive qualities and the lush world that director James Cameron had created. The film was 60 per cent computer-generated and had 2,500 digital effects. It presented a world with landscapes that evoked Roger Dean's Yes album covers from the 1970s and featured intricately designed plant and animal life, striving to appear astonishingly fresh yet at the same time familiar enough to seem authentic. Its use of stereoscopic 3D worked to create a viewing experience similar to the visual and active experience shaped by gaming.

While it is fashionable to take a cynical view of the push to stereoscopic 3D-film releases and see them merely as Hollywood's way of trying to increase revenues and cheat pirates, I believe that many of the *filmmakers* who are exploring the form creatively understand that audiences accustomed to agency in a game world will also be quick to respond to a deeper visual experience in film. This applies particularly to films that rely on fantastical visuals to communicate the narrative convincingly.

Stories that are set in mythical and otherworldly environments have been drivers of digital visual-effects development, and the enduring popularity of these stories has been a boon to the computer-graphics industry. Responding to the demands of visual storytellers in both the games and film industries, computer graphics have been one of the success stories of computerisation. As a result, being able to create photo-realistic images of imagined worlds is as persuasive to us now as was perspective drawing in revolutionising the visual arts five hundred years ago. Whether these photo-realistic or stylised images are presented as a place where a crafted narrative unfolds (as in a filmed version of a story), or whether they are offered to us as a place to play out a narrative through our own agency, so long as we are engaged by that place and by the premise that takes us there, we will spend time in it.

In a sign of the change underway, in a recent interview, film director Peter Jackson remarked that he is currently enjoying playing games more than making films.[23] The evolution of games as a narrative space is proving attractive to all kinds of visual storytellers. Even in a tightly directed game that restricts agency, there is always a sense of exploring the world on offer and this opportunity to create an engaging story world is most attractive to storytellers.

Games developers know that—fairly or unfairly— their games will be judged by the quality of the graphics. The visual style is of paramount importance in marking out the game space for players and giving it a unique sense of place and emotional connection. With these visually-powerful worlds now enhancing the complexity of action that can be undertaken, it is no wonder that games are a rising narrative form.

The 'just do it' generation grew up in what Mark Pesce calls the 'playful world', one in which toys talk back and play guessing games, teaching everything from arithmetic to spelling.[24] We are engaged by visually-compelling, multi-layered media that respond to our personal interaction with them. We want to be able to choose how to explore the 'text' on offer, and tailor it to our particular needs. It is a big universe, this connected world, and it lets us all shine in our own way. We form our own constellations in a networked world and this change informs our expectations of the world around us.

Another factor signalling the elevation of games from 'toy box' to 'art form' is the interest being taken by the academy. In a session at the SIGGRAPH conference mentioned earlier, the 'art history of games' was explored by academics from Savannah College of Art & Design and Georgia Tech. In a scholarly reading of games, they asked questions such as, 'Is the art of games found in the visual elements?' and 'Is the art of games found in the game design?' At this early stage in the evolution of games narratives, they came to few conclusions. However, it is significant that games are being analysed in much the same way as film was in the 1950s and '60s. And, as it took film some forty years to be taken seriously, perhaps we can anticipate that games are now poised for the same kind of scholarly acceptance.

These discussions are taking place outside the academy also. Last April, Roger Ebert weighed in with the view that games will never be as artistically worthy as films.[25] However, it should be noted that it took the talents of great cinematographers and artists such as Hans Geiger, Ron Cobb and generations of classically trained artists drawn to directing and digital visual effects to provide film with the visual power that earned its status as 'art'. So it is perfectly proper for SIGGRAPH panellist Peter Weishar to take up the issue of the art of games by tracing the history of their visual style from the 1990s to the present.

In that session, it was Weishar's contention that much was lost when games became driven by action and art became ancillary to the game. I understand the point he was making, but there are many games that contribute to art through visual style; visual styles that are, in turn, informing the art of film. If we consider this issue in the broader context of 'digital art', which *is* recognized by the art world, then it is fairly straightforward to see that the representational qualities of games are a natural extension of this tradition. Of particular interest is the way games offer players the opportunity to place themselves within imagined worlds and explore ideas of presence and place, ideas that are fundamental to our appreciation of art across many forms.

There is a move in games design towards greater stylisation, which I believe will address Weishar's criticisms. One factor that supports his view is that, while pursing a more 'filmic' approach, games have tended to emulate the photo-realism of film. Ironically, in the meantime, films such as *Speedracer* (a live action and computer-generated film based on a cell animation television series from the 1960s which in itself was based on a Japanese manga series), *300* and *Sin City*, (both based on Frank Miller's graphic novels, the first of which is a retelling of the Battle of Thermopylae, and the latter a noir crime drama set in the fictional Basin City), have been exploring the visual style of graphic novels and games, and have been redefining the representational art of film. This is hardly a surprising development, given that some of the best art talents of our time are working in computer graphics in both games and film. The acceptance of the art of film, and the move to extend this acceptance to games, is part of a maturation of narrative forms that arises from the narrative experience of our most recent generations. What we can look forward to next is how our technological advances will let us go even further.

4

Rebirth of the cool: nurturing new voices

While the technology used to craft innovative artistic achievements might be new, these new works are as inseparable from what came before as we are from the DNA of our forebears. As David Bordwell put it, 'Nothing comes from nothing. Every new artistic achievement revises existing practices, and often the "unconventional" strategy simply draws on *other* conventions.'[26]

In 2007, the Sydney Film Festival screened Paul Robertson's 12-minute animation, *Pirate Baby's Cabana Battle Street Fight*, in which two male characters must fight their way through a building full of humans, zombies and giant grubs to rescue a woman held captive by a baby pirate.[27] It was included in a 'digital strand' on the basis that digital technology had been used to craft some aspect of the work; a criterion that probably covered every other new film in the festival program too. That said, it was an exemplar of the 'digital' in a way that the criteria did not anticipate.

What distinguished Robertson's film was demonstrated by the audience reaction: most of the screenings' attendees were young and they recognised immediately the side-scrolling visual style and gamer conventions upon which the film's content and visual style was based. Fundamentally its narrative origins were games. It was a huge hit, yet I suspect that for those who had never played a side-scrolling platformer, much of what appeared on the screen was a mystery. Visually arresting, but a mystery no less.

For the children of media-wealthy cultures, playing creatively with the media materials of their world is a natural step. Currently, a popular way to make a film is to re-work 'found' materials, transforming the source elements into a different 'text' with its own, new meaning. The now infamous 'Hitler' films posted to YouTube are a great example of this.[28] These short parodies of modern tribulations use a brief excerpt from Constantin Films' *The Downfall* and they inspire a stream of new versions, in defiance of the production company's take-down notices. Another popular form is that of trailer mash-ups, which take film trailers and recast the footage in a new light. The reworking of Nora Ephron's romantic comedy *Sleepless in Seattle* as a trailer for a horror movie, or of Stanley Kubrick's celebrated horror film, *The Shining* remade as a romantic comedy, are particularly good examples.

While many of these works are considered to trespass on copyright (as the *Downfall* example highlights), others have either the tacit or explicit support of IP holders whose works are 'borrowed'. When *Red vs. Blue* (or *RvB*), first circulated—a machinima (i.e. a recording made entirely with games engines and characters) created by Rooster Teeth Productions that uses the science-fiction *Halo* gameplay—there was robust debate as to whether Rooster Teeth would be sued by Microsoft for breach of copyright. However, Microsoft chose to see the productions as an amicable extension of the *Halo* storyworld, a decision that showed an acute understanding of their audience and of the mores of online culture.

Another rising form of production, the 'filmed life' videos on the Internet, also emerges from the heritage of experimental 'diary films' and is a reasonable extension of the perception of self as agent in story. The camera is the ever-present BFF (text-speak for 'best friend forever') or perhaps 'frenemy' of modern society, reworking Socrates' idea of the examined life in a radically new way. The ubiquity of cameras triggers a level of self-as-performer and world-as-image bank that is only beginning to be tapped.

At the 2009 SIGGRAPH conference, MIT, Carnegie Mellon University and the University of Washington academics examined the magnitude of this change in the session, 'The Next Billion Cameras'. Noting that back in 2002 very few mobile phones had cameras, they revealed that by 2008 there were over one billion in use. They then outlined the implications of this phenomenon for visual communication in a world with billions of cameras and billions of images that can be searched, manipulated and re-presented.

As visual communication undergoes this massive change, we are taking up the resources of this growing database of image, performance, and story. The Internet offers many communities of practice, some more formal than others, and many of which are the foundations of advances that we will enjoy in the future. Flickr, a photographic community of practice, provides opportunity for feedback and for the formation of an evolving, ongoing exhibition of related works through themed groups. It also provides an extensive resource for the kinds of technologies the 'Next Billion Cameras' session showcased. By accessing thousands of photographs on Flickr, 3D models of famous buildings and public places were created as part of the demonstration, models that could then, in their turn, be manipulated as the basis for a new work.[29]

Other communities are using the networking and feedback potential of the Internet in order to build repertoire and performances to create original works. It is clear that many of these works are undertaken with indifference to the commercial imperative, while others are crafted with a view to building a following on what are becoming 'TV channels' on YouTube. This blurring of the 'professional' and the 'amateur' is disconcerting in a commodified world and especially testing for those who look to the Internet to define a business model that they can control and contain. For the vast majority of content makers what is most at issue is the opportunity to practise, to refine and to share, practices that are fundamental to online culture.

That said, user-generated content is only one aspect of this new jewel in our creative tiara. There are other ways in which the exchange of conventions between new digital tools and emerging forms has enriched performance, art and film.

Computer graphics and games have been very much about extending performance and the camera. In the last decade, computer-graphics tools have allowed us to capture performance beyond photographic means through technology that captures motion and performance (commonly referred to as 'mocap') and records fine nuances of human movement and expression. Developed extensively by the games industry, this is now a common tool for filmmakers. In games, mocap performance informs the agency available to players and draws on performances by dancers, actors and athletes. While games performance is often dismissed as mere 'play', I would argue that the move to record performance within games and, indeed, to script performance within games for recording, brings it closer to acting. Furthermore, these uses are creating tools that open up performance across different forms and create new kinds of opportunity.

Mocap 'captures' the essence of an actor's physical and facial expressions. The action thus recorded is used to imbue the performances of objects, creatures and other representations, and endow the computer-generated characters and objects with the authentic essence of the human performer's corporeality and of their emotional and physical expressions.

Mocap performances have provided some of the great moments in acting in recent films, including Gollum, King Kong, the *Happy Feet* penguins, the performances in *Beowulf* and those of the Na'vi of *Avatar*. Indeed, director James Cameron has said of *Avatar*: 'The thing I hope the media can convey to audiences is that this is an actor-driven process. Nayteri, in my film for example—she is what Zoe [Saldana] created 100 per cent.'[30]

Cameron's use of head-mounted cameras to record expressions through performance-capture technology pushed back the boundaries of mocap still further and allowed, as theatre director Lee Lewis has written, 'performance that transcends the physical limits of race [...] to represent universal experience.'[31] While Lewis was speaking of the 'entitlement' claimed by Sydney theatre directors to cast white performers in any role, regardless of its apparent racial or ethnic suitability, mocap really does transcend visible attributes, allowing performers to cast off many of the limits set by physical appearance. It lets their bodies become a performance vehicle that can show the real heart driving the emotional expression inherent in a digital face.

An industry long dominated by the beautiful or the camera-loved is making room for the wonderfully expressive. The fat dancer is no longer banished from the stage. The young spirit in the older performer plays on, all the more strongly for the depth of experience that they are able to bring to the role. The digital disguise that mocap provides extends performance, putting aside matters of age and race although not, it seems, gender. We are hardwired to read gender in movement and the integrity of mocap performances is such that it reveals gender in even the most rudimentary wireframe skeletons that underpin the animations we see in finished form. Such is its power to convey the 'human truth' in animated performance.

Fundamentally, however, mocap translates performance into data, data that can be used, extended and modified to suit a director's creative vision. Of course, this throws up new conundrums. When nominations for the Academy Awards opened for the 2010 ceremony, James Cameron reportedly felt that his *Avatar* actors' performances had been mistaken for mere animations, rather than the 'real' thing. Yet animators do extensive work on mocap performances also and they, equally, feel snubbed when their contributions to filmed performances are not recognised.

This is all part of the blurring of traditional performance, to which the use of digital tools gives rise. Will camera moves and lighting, all set by the animatic and undertaken by computer graphics artists using software tools, ever be given a Best Cinematography award? Will the creators of digital environments and costumes be recognised for their production design? We might also ask: will machinima ever be accorded status on a par with that of traditional cinema?

There are other initiatives underway that will extend the definition and range of what constitutes cinema. The University of New South Wales has created an immersive screen environment to explore the potential of narrative, visualisation, interface and interaction.[32] Called iCinema, it is a space that, among other things, surrounds the viewer with imagery and seeks to create an atmosphere of presence within the projected environment. In time, the technical advances that iCinema is looking to achieve will allow us to walk through narrative spaces with the immediacy that compares with our experience in the physical world. A variety of headset technologies and holographic projection systems have similar aims. These are currently being trialled, and if successful will make the stereoscopic 3D productions of today stepping stones to the holodeck of the future.[33]

It is from seeds of change such as these that new forms will grow, shaped by the conventions and expectations that derive from a century of filmmaking and several decades of game development. What will these new forms need? One thing is certain, the future will depend on more than our creativity as storytellers. There are important computing and distribution infrastructure issues that will need to be solved in order to fulfil the potential within our reach. What is concerning, however, is the fact that the needs of the creative industries seem peripheral to the decisions being made about our future playing spaces.

5

Clouds on the horizon vs. rain in a time of drought

How well-equipped and entitled will we be to share in the coming changes? While to date text has dominated the Internet, Cisco Systems estimates that by 2013 video will account for 90 per cent of all Internet traffic.[34] The emergence of new devices, and myriad applications for those devices, will remove even more barriers to creativity and will re-form many of our current narrative products, increasing the infrastructure needs we will have in order both to enjoy and to share our creations.

After years of speculation, ePublishing is being given serious *creative* consideration. Penguin has announced that they will embed audio, video and streaming into the eBook format. As someone who makes a lot of references to films, I would like to see my books linked directly to the films, texts and web resources that I cite. Surely, consumers too would welcome the facility of text multi-layered with video and interactive metadata. I imagine the producers of those referenced works would be even happier, if there were 'buy now' options embedded in those links.

Cinema screens that number in the thousands today compete with billions of device screens that, regardless of the arguments about their inferiority, are being used to view everything we currently know as film, TV, and e-book versions of novels. What will happen when these 'forms' merge and layer themselves in ways that can be explored, modified and shared?

This shift will allow storytellers to draw on a vast range of options to tell their stories; and in a fair world, a range less limited by existing business models and one that will lead to new models that better reward and acknowledge the creators of story and the elements that make up the media in which story is expressed. This might mean that actors and animators will be jointly recognised and royalty-rewarded for their performances, and that production designers and concept artists will be recognised in the production chain that flows into merchandising.

It has been a long journey from the magic lantern to the digital camera/edit suite and YouTube. As we have seen within film, independent filmmakers have struggled to have their stories seen and heard. We must heed these lessons when we shape a future that will rely upon an infrastructure of connectivity and collaborative work. We must insist on a system of financial acknowledgment for creators, rather than reserve the lion's share of rewards for the commercial process that exploits the creative works.

Peter Broderick, with his passion for independent filmmaking and hybrid distribution, is well known to Australian filmmakers. Yet the strategies he endorses and those that will be needed in the future depend on ubiquitous and capacious connectivity. Not just for the forms that we are familiar with now, but, as online content proliferates, for those that are emerging and will shape narrative engagement in the decades ahead. The extent to which these and future needs are being taken into account in our National Broadband Network (NBN) planning is not clear. I am concerned that too much of the focus has been on the commercial aspects of the network and that commentary about the common resource that it needs to become has been, at best, token.

Stuart Cunningham has made an eloquent case for what he calls the 'growth model for creative industries', a model that understands the need to invest in conditions for growth.[35] This is exactly what should be driving the case for the NBN and not just motherhood statements about its importance to our economy. It is fundamentally important that the fibre network is scalable, so that we build for the future and not simply to catch up with other nations and commercial entities that are already ahead in infrastructure. The data-bank issues also need to be considered. Where will our national content resources be stored and how accessible will they be for the creators of the future? What will be our rights to contribute to this digital heritage, and how will we ensure equitable acknowledgement and reward for the contributions made?

We have faced these issues before. In 'From Digital Courier to Global Freight Train', Dominic Case has shown that the Australian industry has not been let down by a lack of vision on the part of Creative Industry players, but by being unable to overcome business case barriers and an unwillingness to invest in 'unjustifiable' infrastructure. As he reminds us, there once was a plan to create an Australian high-speed network to facilitate the exchange of data needed in digital visual effects and post-production. However, because the film and digital visual effects case wasn't lucrative enough, instead of being owners of our own infrastructure, we are customers of someone else's.[36]

The infrastructure requirements for digital content are substantial. At a forum entitled 'Digital Sydney', held in May 2010, Steam Engine CEO Stefan Gillard described the computing power needed for *Avatar*.[37] To give it context, he explained that if he digitised the entire Library of Congress, it would require the same computing infrastructure as *Avatar*, which was only 60 per cent computer-generated. So what will the infrastructure needs be as we move to a 90-per-cent video Internet? Animal Logic, with bases in Sydney and Los Angeles and ranked globally as a leading visual-effects studio, has infrastructure that ranks it among the world's leading supercomputing facilities also.

What does all this mean for emerging storytellers and narrative forms that have yet to be invented? Obviously, it is hard to make a business case for technology and uses that are as yet undefined, but we have to ensure that our potential needs as content creators are accommodated. We know that there are key issues that, if addressed properly, will serve us into the future.

Two things have been significant contributors to the digital revolution. First, many of the tools were adapted for mass consumption. Digital cameras, home computers, image manipulation software, music programs, all have very high quality 'consumer'-standard products. The professional flatbed editing suites of the past rarely graced the average family home, but today anyone with an iMac has iMovie bundled with the purchase and filmmaking is a primary-school activity like diorama making and crayoning. This access to production tools is fundamental to the changes we are seeing and the expectations people have about their rights as creators.

The second significant contributor is the open-access policy that has been inherent in the development and roll-out of the Internet. The Internet was not made by and for the hands of the few: it is a tool of the many. Once computers and telecommunications networks were brought together, the starting gun was fired and it was 'game on', and the game included everyone who entered the field of play. This is not a situation that makes the oligopoly happy. As we have seen in the film industry, creativity flourishes best when access is widened. Conversely, when any industry is dominated by only a few players, innovation suffers and choice becomes the prerogative of the controllers of production.

Currently, we are poised to provide ubiquitous access to means of production and publishing, unless we lose this latest battle for corporate control by allowing entrenched players to gain dominance over the new playing fields. The problem is that too many of those making decisions about the Internet can only imagine what they already know and have a vested interest in maintaining the status quo. They are the kind of people who suffer the shock of the new and find it threatening.

The Net neutrality debate focuses on three key areas.[38] The first is the matter of anti-competitive practices. In a discussion of these issues, Columbia University law professor Tim Wu noted:

> In the early days of mobile phones, the only way an application appeared on a mobile phone was if it made money for the phone company. [...] In an Internet that [ISPs] can control, why would you put Wikipedia on it? It doesn't make sense because it doesn't make money.[39]

And this is the crux of the issue: *The Internet wasn't created as a commercial enterprise.* Nevertheless, many communications companies now want to 'own' it and governments want to 'regulate' it in line with their own priorities.

In March 2010, in an address to the Congressional-Executive Commission on China, Google argued that censorship was not only a human rights issue, but a marketplace concern because it stifled innovation.[40] This is something that we have seen happen before. In his discussion of how monopolies were established over technologies, Brian Winston traces the trajectory of the gradual industrialisation and politicisation of artisan newspapers in Britain:

> By the middle years of the 19th century, newspapers had transformed themselves from small-scale enterprises with uncontrollable and unpredictable political and social effects into large, capital-intensive operations, belonging to and controlled by

a class of citizen concerned both to make profits and to exercise social control in favour of the established order.[41]

One of the political advantages of having control in the hands of a few key players in an industry is that it is much easier to negotiate deals with them. This is another pattern that repeats itself throughout history, with power, financial reward, and control over production devolving to a small group that vests interests in the success of its members, usually at the expense of those who are not its members.

While a powerful tool in the hands of the many, the Internet presents an enormous threat to the whole, should its control wind up in the hands of the few, because the capacity to use it as a tool for oppression is immense. It is a double-edged sword: freedom if it cuts one way, tyranny if it cuts the other. If, as the network grows, anti-competitive practices become entrenched, then we will be in trouble, and the renaissance in form and content that we enjoy now and anticipate into the future will be greatly delayed, if not stillborn.

This is unlikely to happen overnight. Positions of monopoly or oligopoly usually develop over time, often facilitated by the second Net neutrality issue: the creation of hierarchies in which elite groups have preferential access and privileges. There are many ways to introduce this, one of the most popular means being fee-structuring, whereby the rich pay and the poor do without. This is often referred to as the 'digital divide', with an emerging class of digitally-equipped citizens having advantages over those who do not have the resources to avail themselves of digital tools. This is an ironic turn, given that digital technologies have trended toward opening accessibility as they became affordable and a wealth of creativity has ensued.

In terms of the Internet, the obligation as it stands now is that Internet traffic does not have 'special lanes'. For the most part there is no differentiation in access and transfer on the basis of a 'class system' of users (obviously there are private networks, but the public Internet is still open to all). This ensures that everyone who is on the system is pretty much able to get the same advantages. However, it would be simplicity itself to change that and commercial operators would see distinct advantages in being able to create such hierarchies within their customer bases.

The creation of fee-for-freedom 'classification' systems, and a failure to provide infrastructure unless it meets commercial case standards, are all means by which entrenched players seek to limit entry to the field of play.

By way of example, in the fallout over the Bill Henson exhibit in 2008, a new process came into effect in Australia permitting the classification of photographs—for a fee per image. Ostensibly, this classification system provides artists with validation of their works so as to avoid prosecution for pornography. This sounds reasonable enough, until you reflect that it is essentially a tax on creativity and yet another price for entry into exhibiting creative works. Not so onerous for those with deep pockets, but certainly sufficient to inhibit those without. We should note that the debate about Henson's photographs started with an image posted on a gallery's website. Currently, the Internet lets anyone post images to sites such as Flickr or Facebook, with very little regulation. How long will it be before someone gets the bright idea that each image will need to be 'classified'? This leads to the third major issue: censorship.

Many—often politicians—will argue that the elected government of a free and democratic society would *never dare* use Internet filtering to control information and that political bias would *never* dictate to artists the nature of their creative output. Yet history shows that there have been repeated instances of precisely this. In *A New Pot of Gold: Hollywood under the Electronic Rainbow, 1980–1989*,[42] film historian Stephen Prince documents Ronald Reagan's slow dismantling of the funding for the National Endowment for the Humanities over the course of the 1980s. One of the significant policy decisions was to prohibit funding for any documentary with explicit political content.

As this example from the USA and Brian Winston's of newspapers in the UK show, if these two nations have managed to curtail citizens' freedoms, why should Australians accept the word of their political and corporate masters when they claim that the natural safeguards of an educated populace in a modern democracy will be sufficient in the face of secret blacklists?

According to Clay Shirky, 'With the arrival of globally accessible publishing, freedom of speech is now freedom of the press, and freedom of the press is freedom of assembly.' He adds later: 'The pro-freedom argument does not imply a society without regulations.'[43] However, the philosophy that underpins a regulatory framework must be based on respect for its citizens and their freedoms.

As so much of the discussion on Internet censorship has focussed on emotive issues of child safety, I'm going to digress for a moment to provide an example of the difference between a permissive philosophy and repressive philosophy. A permissive philosophy is one in which, unless explicitly stated otherwise, one can assume that the right to act rests with the individual. In a repressive philosophy, rights do not exist unless they have been granted; in effect, if you want to do something, you must first obtain permission to do so.

In Sydney, there is a very common and, virtually, daily opportunity to see the difference in these two regulatory stances in action. Unless a sign tells us we can make a left-hand turn on a red traffic light, in Sydney we are not permitted to do so. Secondly, unless pedestrians have pressed the button on the lights, they will not get a green light for safe crossing. Elsewhere, the rules allow that you may turn on the red light (unless a sign prohibits it) and pedestrian lights automatically permit crossing as a priority; there is no need to seek permission first by pressing a button. The next time you wait for the lights in Sydney, think about the psychology of behaviour modification.

What does any of this have to do with censorship? I think it stands as an analogy for a particular mindset, one that says, 'If you haven't been granted permission, you are *not* allowed to proceed.' This philosophy can have influence in all kinds of regulation, policy, and service delivery, and its prevalence can lead to that most insidious of all forms of censorship: self-censorship, and the belief that your rights are very limited, a state that might be described as oppressive.

I once participated in a discussion about Internet Protocol TV (on-demand access to commercial content libraries over the Internet). The invited speaker had described developments in the USA to provide this through cable and download subscription models. An Australian observer, after confirming that this model was 'for real', shook his head and said: 'Oh, we'll never be allowed to have that *here*.' Someone from a television network promptly agreed, asserting that delivery of content over the Internet was not what Australian audiences wanted, that they did not want to have to 'dig around on the Internet' when there were trusted network broadcasters to make their choices for them.

The issue of censorship has always shadowed the arts. Unlike Peter Pan, we cannot be separated from this shadow, as it is in the very nature of the arts to challenge the status quo, to question the presumptions of society, and to encourage debate, discussion and dissent. Yet, increasingly, the arts are being subjected to homogenisation and sanitisation. Being 'offensive', it would seem, is more frightening than censorship, corruption or injustice. There is a view that we should protect people from depictions of 'wrong' or 'inappropriate' behaviour, yet the imposition on writers, filmmakers, performers, and artists of a requirement to be subservient to sets of constantly shifting values is censorship.

All too often these debates have been overwhelmed by the stench of the red herring: 'How can you oppose our plans? Think of the children.' Should not 'thinking of the children' be as much about protecting their rights to imagine, to learn, and to express their voices in a global digital world?

These issues merit a Platform Paper of their own, but I raise them so that we may consider the imperative that obliges us to fight yet again for the right to speak our minds frankly and fearlessly in our work. There are moves afoot to sneak a repressive regulatory mechanism into Australia's Internet access and while discussion abounds as to whether it will work or not, the key concern is that *it introduces a new tool of censorship* and puts it firmly in the hands of the government and its appointed gatekeepers. Further, it does this by removing an existing freedom from the citizenry.

If the controversial Lenny Bruce were to talk about 'cocksuckers' in a comedy venue today, no-one would bat an eyelid, let alone call the police. He, and the rights movement that followed him, had the courage to stand up and say the unsayable, things that challenged the US laws of the day—that the colour of a person's skin was no measure of their character, for example. As a result, we have enjoyed a level of permissiveness that has made our societies more tolerant, more openly diverse and our cultural outputs have benefited immensely.

The principle that adults have the right to make decisions for themselves as long as they do not curtail the rights of others is one that we like to think prevails. If we want to protect this principal, then we must challenge the plans we see emerging for the Internet.

An organisation committed to the denunciation of human rights violations world-wide, Reporters without Borders, has put Australia on its watch list as a country that is a threat to citizen's freedom of access to the Internet. This is hardly surprising, when the government of the day has consistently shown itself impervious to the raised voices of reason, such as those of former High Court Judge Michael Kirby, the US Ambassador Jeff Bleich, academic experts such as Bjorn Landfeldt, and child protection groups. It dismisses the technical advice of virtually every operator in the field.

As US Ambassador Bleich said, 'We (Americans) have been able to accomplish the goals that Australia has described, which is to capture and prosecute child pornographers [...] without having to use internet filters.'[44] So, if filtering the Internet isn't the way to stop child pornographers, why is Australia's government so determined to institute such a repressive measure?

It is concerning that many of the steps being introduced to establish censorship and regulation go hand-in-hand with the interests of the powerbrokers. As Ambassador Bleich has argued, there is nothing to stop the enactment of strong legal remedies against criminal behaviour in whatever sphere it is undertaken, but—make no mistake about this—it is not the sphere, but the behaviour, that needs be regulated, and the proposed filtering of the Internet is about controlling the sphere.

Censorship by stealth, through quiet and incremental additions of 'refused classification' web addresses that are subject neither to public scrutiny nor transparent means of redress, places enormous power for oppression in the hands of a nameless, faceless few. When such measures come alongside non-competitive market conditions and non-egalitarian business practices, then we face a trifecta of domination that shuts out participation on many levels.

Worryingly, there is too much in the current proposals that demonstrates the extraordinary effort that is going into keeping alive outmoded businesses. This shouldn't be a surprise, since it is the media that control the debate on the future of the media. The entrenched players are using their lobbying powers to influence legislative and regulatory systems to stack the game in their favour and to overturn the most sacred principles of law. In the UK, the Digital Economy Act is reported to require that anyone accused of the illegal downloading of copyrighted materials will have to prove their innocence, in contravention of the principle of 'innocent until proven guilty'.

In a digital world, we have seen the media oligopoly's determination to protect the hierarchy-enforcing and anti-commercial practices of 'windows' and globally differentiated markets and 'regions'. Similarly, movie- and book-release schedules mean that utterly notional boundaries are erected to protect a physical distribution system that suits corporate interests, but not the reality of communication in a connected society. What creative benefit does Australia gain by being excluded from participating in the first-release world's critical analysis? How are local content makers advantaged by having to wait to see the latest works of their colleagues elsewhere?

Information is power. It always has been. Access to knowledge about filmmaking used to be hard to acquire, and this gave a distinct advantage to those who 'owned' the industry. Elizabeth Daley, Dean of the University of Southern California's School of Cinema-Television, has said that, '[t]he greatest digital divide is between those who can read and write with media, and those who can't. Our core knowledge needs to belong to everybody.'[45]

The Internet is the commons of the digital world. Its sites are our boulevards and our galleries and stages. It is 'us'. When Senator Conroy states that the Internet is not special, he could not reveal his government's ignorance of the Internet's potential more eloquently. Like many who put themselves above others, he fails to understand that we are all special. We are the stories. It is *our* participation and creativity that makes the Internet the most exciting creative forum in history.

'The internet does not know what it is being used for', writes Clay Shirky. 'This fact has many ramifications, but two of the most important ones are vanishingly cheap many-to-many communications, and the flexibility that allows people to design and try new communications tools without having to ask anyone for permission.'[46]

There are many in the creative fields who look on digital technologies as 'dull computer stuff' without understanding how important 'that stuff' is to the future of creative works and the capacity to find an audience and be rewarded for creative products.

Too much of what we hear is about the engineering challenge and the commercial case: discussions loaded with technical jargon.

If more of the planning for the future engaged creators and focussed on creating equitable processes for acknowledgment and income streams, perhaps there would be more interest. If the debate about Internet filtering addressed the impact it will have on individual creators and access to legitimate works instead of being allowed to disintegrate into arguments about pornography, then there might be more action. If discussions about piracy and lost royalties led to mechanisms that allow legal satisfaction of consumer demands and micropayment accounting systems that share the wealth fairly, then perhaps we would be closer to a real digital economy.

If building the NBN was given the same scrutiny by the creative community that it would get if it was a centre for the arts, then I think we would be having a quite different debate and we would be seeing a much more effective fight to ensure our futures and preserve our rights. The Internet is our California. When filmmakers were frustrated by the entrenched interests of theatre, of patent holders and cartels, they headed west and made their own town. That spirit of freedom and independence must be brought to creating our new creative spaces. The next evolution in narrative form will be the child of film and games, and it deserves the connected world as its playground.

We see now the audience ready to turn performer, director, and producer. The Goliath of entrenched interests wants to keep things as they are. But the fight is not over. There is still hope. We need to pile up the rocks of our creativity and make ready our slingshots. Are you ready to play to win? Are you ready to cry 'w00t', when the future is yours and you have the freedom to do your best work and share it without getting permission first and without having to censor yourself instead of speaking the truth? If so, take up the rock that is your creativity, and may your aim be true.

Endnotes

1   Gamer speak for 'we own the other team'; i.e. 'we win'. It is also an exclamation of triumph and joy.

2   *So What's This All About, Then: A Non-User's Guide to Digital Effects in Filmmaking* (Sydney: AFTRS, 1998).

3   *The Satchel—Production Budgeting and Film Management*, available at http://www.screenaustralia.gov.au/filming_in_australia/budgeting/satchel.asp (accessed 20 May 2010).

4   *Digital Storytelling: The Narrative Power of Visual Effects in Film.* (Cambridge, Mass.: MIT Press, 2007).

5   *Technologies of Seeing: Photography, Cinematography and Television* (London: BFI, 1996), p.3.

6   *The Way Hollywood Tells It* (Berkeley: University of California Press, 2006), pp.1–18.

7   *The Way Hollywood Tells It*, p.4.

8   Bordwell, p.3.

9   *How Hollywood Works* (London: SAGE Publications, 2003), p.60.

10 'Murdoch's Plan for Paywall Success: Readers Will Pay "When They've Got Nowhere Else to Go"', available at http://paidcontent.org/article/419-murdochs-plan-for-paywall-success-readers-will-pay-when-they've-got-nowhere-else-to-go (accessed 11 April 2010).

11 Alexander Aciman and Emmett Rensin, *Twitterature* (Harmondsworth: Penguin, 2009), pp.27–9.

12 *The Uses of Enchantment: The Meaning and Importance of Fairy Tales* (Harmondsworth: Penguin, 1991), p.10.

13   *The Way Hollywood Tells It*, p.59.

14   'Telling Tales: The Evolutions of Four Stories', *Lapham's Quarterly*, Spring, 2010, available at http://laphamsquarterly.org/ (accessed 20 April 2010).

15   By Pierre Corneille in 1659, Voltaire in 1718, La Motte in 1726, Ducis in 1778 and Jules Lacroix in 1858.

16   See the project website at http://www.starwarsuncut.com/ and the trailer at http://vimeo.com/10821312 (accessed 11 May 2010).

17   *Here Comes Everybody: How Change Happens When People Come Together* (Harmondsworth: Penguin, 2008), p.21.

18   'One More User, Team Fortress 2— Law-Abiding Engineer', available at http://www.youtube.com/watch?v=HjGrHBpfqCo (accessed 13 May 2010).

19   Post dated 11 March 2010, *The Escapist* online magazine, available at http://www.escapistmagazine.com/articles/view/columns/on-the-ball/7272-On-the-Ball-Two-Shooters (accessed 19 March 2010).

20   For statistics, see http:// www,grabstats,cin/statcatergorymain.asp?StatCatID=13 and http://vgsales.wikia.com/wiki/Video_game_industry, also the US Census Bureau, International Database (accessed 7April 2010).

21   See http://gdaa.com.au/about (accessed 7 April 2010).

22   See sources cited in n. 20 above.

23   See 'Jackson bucks the trend in play-it-safe Hollywood', *Sydney Morning Herald*, 12 December 2009, available at http://www.smh.com.au/cgi- (accessed 20 May 2010).

24   *The Playful World: How Technology is Transforming our Imagination* (New York: Ballantine, 2000).

25   'Video games can never be art', in Ebert's Journal/blogs.suntimes.com (accessed 16 April 2010).

26   *The Way Hollywood Tells It*, p.76.

27   This film can be seen at http://www.youtube.com/watch?v=T5zpNfTfGZU0 (accessed 6 May 2010).

28   At the time of writing, Constantin Films had taken the view that these parodies were a breach of copyright and had issued orders that they be removed from YouTube. Constantin Films was at once the subject of considerable and global animosity, with many commentators encouraging the creators of the parodies to force Constantin to take them to court, where a Fair Use case could be argued in support of the parodies. Within hours of the take-down orders being issued, creators had made new *Downfall* parodies using the clip—in which Hitler screams in frustration and anger about their behaviour—to mock Constantin's decision,. In the meantime, the parodies continue to be made and uploaded to YouTube: see http://www.youtube.com/watch?v=QSYk8ofhYFY (accessed 12 May 2010).

29   The conference presenters were Ramesh Raskar (speaking on 'Cameras of the Future'), Steve Seitz (on 'Reconstruction of the World'), and Aleysha Efros (on 'Understanding a Billion Photos').

30   Cited in 'It's about Storytelling. It's about Humans Playing Humans', posted 21 December 2009 and available at http://www.slate.com/ (accessed 20 May 2010).

31   *Cross-racial Casting: Changing the Face of Australian Theatre*, Platform Papers 13 (Sydney: Currency House: 2007), p.35.

32   See http://www.icinema.unsw.edu.au/ (accessed 12 May 2010).

33   The holodeck is a fictionalised version of a simulated reality facility that features in the *Star Trek* franchise. It is a place where participants can choose an interactive and realistic narrative experience that responds to their actions.

34   Erick Schonfeld, 'Cicso: By 2013 Video will be 90 per cent of all consumer IP traffic and 64 per

cent of Mobile.' Available at http://techcrunch. com/2009/06/09/cisco-by-2013-video-will-be-90-percent-of-all-consumer-ip-traffic-and-64-percent-of-mobile/ (accessed 15 May 2010).

35   In a presentation at 'Digital Sydney', a New South Wales Government Department of Industry and Investment workshop, on 12 May 2010.

36   See *content+technology*, 7.1 (February 2010), pp.14–6.

37   In a presentation at 'Digital Sydney', a New South Wales Government Department of Industry and Investment workshop, on 12 May 2010.

38   See Alan Joch, 'Debating Net Neutrality', *Communications of the ACM*, 52.10 (2009), pp.14-5.

39   Cited in Joch, pp.14–5.

40   See Javier C. Hernandez, 'Google calls for action on web limits', *New York Times*, 24 March 2010.

41   *Technologies of Seeing*, p.27.

42   (Berkeley: University of California Press, 2000), p.373.

43   *Here Comes Everybody*, pp.171, 305.

44   Asher Moses, 'US ambassador slams Conroy's filters' *Sydney Morning Herald*, 13 April 2010.

45   Elizabeth Van Ness, 'Is a Cinema Studies degree the new MBA?', *New York Times*, 6 March 2005.

46   *Here Comes Everybody*, pp.157–8.

Readers' Forum

Responses to James Waites' *Whatever Happened to the STC Actors Company?*, (Platform Papers 23)

George Ogilvie, who was a founding director of the Melbourne Theatre Company, has directed either theatre or opera or ballet for every one of Australia's major performing arts companies.

Whatever Happened to the STC Actors Company? is a meticulously researched paper by James Waites that recounts the sad history of a major theatre project that left behind 'a glitter of fabulous memories', but was ultimately less than it might have been. As someone who has spent almost sixty years in the Australian theatre, as both actor and director, I was keen to read this essay. Having done so, however, I was left with a fundamental question unanswered: Why was the Actors Company formed in the first place?

It is useless asking an actor why s/he is an actor. S/he will seldom know why they are prepared to spend their lives prostituting their god-given talent for becoming someone else. Nor are most theatre directors able to give a more satisfactory reason for doing what they do, unless it be that they 'love working with actors', 'bringing the great classical texts off the page' or 'making audiences laugh or cry'.

However, when it comes to the formation of an 'extension company', a new addition to an already long-established theatre company, a serious answer is required: an idea, concept, philosophy, a *raison d'être* is vital. Something better than 'to put on a number of plays' is needed as justification for binding a dozen highly individual and talented actors together for several years. Mr Waites describes in detail the individuals connected with the STC project, but nowhere, it seems, was there ever a central philosophy that bound them all together at the outset, or (as Dan Spielman hoped) that emerged as they embarked on their work.

'Ensemble' is a term much bandied about in the theatre world. It is a term that implies a project of some kind that has brought actors and directors together and that drives them all towards the same goal. This justification usually comes from the heart and mind of a single initiator, or else from those of the participants (who may be selected on the basis of their suitability). Perhaps the most famous ensemble in the last hundred years of Western theatre has been the Berliner Ensemble, whose founding father was Bertolt Brecht and whose function was the production of Brecht's very particular 'epic' form of political theatre. There have been others, of course, as Mr Waites notes, both elsewhere and in Australia. I often think back to the vision of (the greatly missed) Rex Cramphorn and his (wickedly underfunded) company's tightly focussed Shakespeare project. Different as all these ensembles have been, what they had in common was a unifying goal. That goal might have been, like Brecht's, the translation into theatrical terms of a Marxist ideology. But it could as readily be the use of mask; stage narrative, the telling of epic tales; an exploration of mime; comic playing, from farce to high comedy of manners; unknown European classics (the drama of Golden Age Spain, for example); forgotten Australian plays ... the list is endless.

The STC did not use the term 'ensemble', but called its actors and directors an 'Actors Company', implying that the actors or that acting was the point of the operation. But I don't think that is enough. Actors compose all spoken drama companies (except puppet companies) and we presume that somehow the exploration of different modes of performance and improvements in acting standards (whatever they are!) are what all theatre companies are about. It seems to me particularly important that there be a specific, clearly defined project—especially when one remembers that the 'mother company' was already a broad community company. (Was the purpose of the Actors Company discussed with Premier Bob Carr and the original funding body?) The STC is a community theatre company and as such its unspoken duty is to serve community taste by presenting a wide-ranging program of plays that both keep it alive and also give it a defined identity. Though they have been doing this for many years, with the ups and downs inevitable in any great city, they seem currently to be seeking to establish for themselves an 'International name' rather than developing a distinctly 'Australian identity.'

When a company has in its ranks a great actress with an international reputation, it seems a pity that the company should have taken coals to Newcastle by taking an American play to America. Why not look to take, say, Ray Lawler's *Summer of the Seventeenth Doll* (with our great actress in the tragic role of Olive), a classic play as important to the Australian psyche as Tennessee Williams' *Streetcar Named Desire* is to the American. Or, as Mr Waites very properly suggests, take the Actors

Company's very fine production of Patrick White's *Season at Sarsaparilla* together with the highly talented Kate Mulvany's *The Seed*, with its Australian experience of Vietnam? It would be an Australian package worth sending to any of the world's great theatre cities. What is the point of this seemingly irrelevant paragraph, you ask. It is to illustrate that such a plan could easily involve *both* companies, and to best advantage. Therefore, what on earth was the intention behind the STC's decision to divide itself in two and create a second 'community theatre' company, with a repertory that the 'mother' company could have presented?

In short, what Mr Waites has brilliantly demonstrated is that not enough thought was put into intentions and goals, and more particularly, that no central idea was offered that would identify the new company as an entity independent of its mother company. This Platform Paper is a timely and important document, and should be required reading for anyone inclined to set up an ensemble company in our country.

George Whaley is an actor, director, writer and teacher. Formerly Head of Acting at NIDA, Head of Directing at AFTRS, Director of University Theatre at Melbourne University, he has been co-founder of two theatre companies. His biography of Leo McKern was published in 2008 by UNSW Press.

Whatever Happened to the STC Actors Company?, James Waites' instructive page-turner, is an essential read for every performing arts professional. Robyn Nevin's ambition for a Sydney Theatre Company acting ensemble and its eventual realisation has everything required of an engrossing melodrama: an inspirational vision, wealthy benefactors, philosophical differences, internecine conflict, high expectations, suspense, triumph—and disappointment and regret as the vision dimmed. It also has a great cast of characters.

The author's title is a question that he does his best to answer. If he does not quite succeed it is for reasons he knows and we can guess. Meanwhile, a few hungry pachyderms loiter in the prompt corner, unfed except by gossip, innuendo and blame. This is not helpful.

All theatre companies should be ensembles, as indeed, many are and have long been, worldwide. An ensemble's guiding principle, in the *Macquarie Dictionary*'s admirably clear definition, is that 'each part is considered only in relation to the whole'. Theatrically speaking, ensemble is the antithesis of the star system, in which satellite actors orbit the incandescent star who must always be the centre of attention. In these days of celebrity and individualism, when fame ranks more highly than excellence, a revival of the ensemble ideal is well worth fighting for. The perceived 'failure' of the Actors Company will, doubtless, provide ammunition to those who should know better, who believe that an ensemble company is neither desirable nor affordable. (And there are others, in suits and the screen trades, who believe that rehearsal is neither necessary nor affordable. But that's a debilitating story for another occasion.)

The Actors Company's high aims may not have been fully realised, but they did present some high-quality theatre. Waites' final paragraph reads: 'Examined from close up, as this essay has done, the story of the AC is fraught with set-backs and trauma. Seen from the distance of the stalls and in hindsight, however, it is a glitter of fabulous memories.' That's high praise indeed, and comes from an honest and informed theatre critic appreciated by readers, if not always by theatre managements, for his fearless probing.

What's so good about an ensemble? The short answer is: the quality of the work is enhanced. Ensemble actors play for each other, not primarily for either the audience or the camera. The resulting quality of communion between characters draws the audience into the interrelationships and, therefore, the story. Ensemble involves a commitment to, and insists on creating time for, in-depth exploration of the internal and external details of character and story—and the sharing of common objectives. These principles and qualities are the hallmark of ensemble acting. Ensemble actors and directors worthy of the name are team-players, and at their best have an edge, a dynamic, a quality of danger and unpredictability. They do not woo, nor do they aim to charm: their focus and the detail they give their work demand the audience's attention. The ensemble is a place for exploration and experiment; it must never be a sheltered workshop for time-servers.

But is an Australian ensemble possible—at a time when the art-theatre companies are living beyond their means and seeking more government subsidies and private and corporate sponsorships? And when more and more actors are longing for Hollywood, as a generation earlier they had longed for London—or at least for a local television series or movie—rather than a long-term commitment to working in an ensemble?

The answers, in my opinion, are yes and yes! It is affordable, or the Sydney Theatre Company would not have formed another ensemble, this time of younger actors, called The Residents—not, the 'Holy Twelve', as Waites calls the Nevin's ensemble, or 'the best of the best'. This latter appellation is both offensive and silly. There is no such thing. Acting is not an Olympic sport: there is no 'best'. A dozen directors, critics, theatregoers or actors would each make a different list of their preferred ensemble members—which, by the way, should always include a director or and actor-director or two—with playwrights specially commissioned to develop works for and, importantly, with the ensemble.

I believe that the subsidised companies should *be* ensembles, and not *have* ensembles. If they claim that more funding would be needed for that to be feasible, let them look to their payrolls and lists of offstage employees. A reordering of priorities might be in order.

If more taxpayers' money is to be spent, it should be for the development of lean, independent, alternative ensemble companies—unencumbered by 'national theatre' additions and expensive real estate. Variety is the lifeblood of the performing arts; paucity of choice is their death. The generally timid repertoire currently offered by the subsidised drama theatre companies to the few who can afford their ticket-prices is determined by about a dozen individuals nation-wide, individuals who also decide who will direct, design and act in the productions. This concentrates too much power in the hands of too few. And worse: most of this elite cabal will remain glued to their office chairs long past their use-by dates. Current audiences are being short-changed and potential audiences deterred. Safe programming and long-term enthronements can result in organisational sclerosis.

It is said that actors are wary of joining an ensemble. Some are, as was the case with one or two members of the AC, but wariness is not general, if only for economic reasons. Unlike the artistic directors and administrators who hire them, few actors earn a living wage and must rely on casual employment unrelated to their training and skills. The majority of graduates from our many full-time (and part-time) acting academies would leap at the chance to be part of an ensemble that offered, say, one-year contracts. So would the many experienced actors looking for a greater challenge than is offered by the occasional TV commercial or guest role in a soap. As Waites notes, there is a range of different models, from the fixed membership—which perhaps works best when the object of the exercise is the exploration of well-defined program of work (e.g. Rex Cramphorn's Shakespeare Project)—to the core membership model in which the nucleus is joined by 'associate' actors and directors who come and go (e.g. Sydney's Old Tote Theatre Company in its early days).

It might also be objected that audiences get tired of seeing the same actors in play after play. This was not my own experience some decades ago, when I acted and directed in Melbourne's Emerald Hill Theatre and Melbourne Theatre Companies. Nor was it the case with Theatre ACT, which I founded more recently. All of these were ensemble companies. There was little philosophising (not that there's anything wrong with a little philosophy!) and there were some disagreements (aren't there always?) and it was obvious to all involved, including the audiences, that teamwork enhanced the quality of our work, as well as the development of the actors' skills, range and courage. Audiences assumed a sort of 'ownership' of the actors and, far from being bored by regularly seeing the same faces, came to see what their favourite actors were doing 'this time'.

Robyn Nevin's aspirations and James Waites' analysis of them have reopened debate and discussion about the virtues and vicissitudes of ensemble companies. There is more to be said—and Waites (he was *dramaturg* on the Rex Cramphorn project) is both well-placed and well-fitted to the task of writing a comprehensive treatment of the subject. Should he be tempted, I suggest he look at Gus Worby's 1979 doctoral thesis, which he wrote at Flinders University. It's titled 'The Ensemble Ideal and the Australian Theatre, 1956–1966', and it deals in depth with the Emerald Hill Theatre. I have to confess a special interest here: I was co-founder and associate director of the company, which was led by Wal Cherry.